TURN VACUUM ON

PUSH VACUUM

FORWARD

BACK

FORWARD

BACK

TURN 45°

PUSH VACUUM

FORWARD

BACK

FORWARD

BACK

TURN 45°

PUSH VACUUM

FORWARD

BACK

FORWARD

BACK

VACUUM UNDER STUFF

PUSH VACUUM

FORWARD

BACK

FORWARD

BACK

TURN 45°

PUSH VACUUM

FORWARD

BACK

FORWARD

BACK

VACUUM UNDER MORE STUFF

PUSH VACUUM

FORWARD

BACK

FORWARD

BACK

TURN 30°

PUSH VACUUM

FORWARD

BACK

FORWARD

BACK

TURN 30°

PUSH VACUUM

FORWARD

BACK

FORWARD

BACK

TURN VACUUM OFF

PUT VACUUM AWAY

www.ingramcontent.com/pod-product-compliance
Ingram Content Group UK Ltd.
Pitfield, Milton Keynes, MK11 3LW, UK
UKHW022009190726
13853UKWH00004B/1833